TED RUNS AWAY FROM HOME

TED RUNS AWAY FROM HOME
A PICTURE CORGI BOOK 0 552 524832

First published in Great Britain by Hamish Hamilton Children's Books, by arrangement with Borgen, Copenhagen.

PRINTING HISTORY
Hamish Hamilton edition published 1986
Picture Corgi edition published 1988

Picture Corgi Books are published by Transworld Publishers Ltd., 61-63 Uxbridge Road, Ealing, London W5 5SA, in Australia by Transworld Publishers (Australia) Pty. Ltd., 15-23 Helles Avenue, Moorebank, NSW 2170, and in New Zealand by Transworld Publishers (N.Z.) Ltd., Cnr. Moselle and Waipareira Avenues, Henderson, Auckland.

Printed and bound in Portugal by
Printer Portuguesa

Jan Mogensen

Ted Runs Away from Home

PICTURE CORGI

Ted was all alone in the house. Jack and Mary were playing outside. Ted sat on Mary's bed feeling cross. Nobody had spoken to him for three whole days.

"It would serve them right if I was dead," Ted thought. "Then they would wish they hadn't left me alone. I think I'll run away."

Ted got up. "That's it. I'll run away from home!" he declared. "Now, what do I need? Something to carry things in, of course. Right, I'm ready," he said out loud.

First Ted went to the kitchen. “Shall I take something to eat?” he wondered. “No,” he decided. “There is no time to lose.” He peeped through the open door. “All clear!”

Ted saw the ladder that led up to the attic. "I'll go this way," he said to himself. "Nobody will find me up here." Ted had to stop and rest half way up. "Running away is very tiring," he thought.

When Ted reached the top of the ladder, he pushed the door with all his strength. The attic was rather dark and dusty. It was also *very* quiet.

Then, suddenly, Ted heard a voice say, "Would anyone like more tea?"

RA
TION

"Is anybody there?" Ted asked timidly. Quietly he crept towards the sound of voices.

In a broken-down old doll's house he saw a toy soldier, a doll with a bow in her hair, and a clockwork mouse. They were having tea and talking. They did not see Ted.

Ted coughed and said, "How do you do?"

PARIS

The soldier, the doll and the clockwork mouse got such a fright, they leapt to their feet. The soldier jumped right out of the doll's house and landed in Ted's arms.

"I do beg your pardon," the soldier said, standing to attention and saluting Ted. "We thought you were a mouse."

"No, I'm Ted," said Ted.

"We have a lot of trouble with wild mice," the doll explained, "especially at night. Would you like a cup of tea?"

Ted sat down at the table. "I've run away from home," he told the others. "Have you?"
"What does that mean?" asked the soldier.
"Well, don't you usually live with the children?" said Ted.
"Children? What are children?" the soldier, the doll and the clockwork mouse asked together. "You must remember, we have been here for a very long time. Perhaps we have forgotten."
"Children are people who play with you – when they remember," Ted explained.
"Oh yes, I think I remember," said the doll. "And they dress you up, don't they?"
"And they wind me up," said the clockwork mouse. "Or they used to," she added sadly.

So Ted, the soldier, the doll and the clockwork mouse sat and talked about the children.

"Do you have children at home Ted?" asked the soldier.

Ted, remembering Jack and Mary, decided he did not want to run away at all; in fact he wanted to go home right away.

He got up. "Thank you for tea," he said. They waved sadly goodbye and Ted went to the top of the stairs. Then he had an idea, "Do you want to come with me?" he asked.

When, a little later, Jack and Mary came in from the garden, they saw the three dolls sitting at the top of the stairs.

"Look," Jack called. "I wonder where they came from. Let's clean them up."

"I wonder if we can make the clockwork mouse work," Mary said.

By teatime, the soldier had a brand new sword, the doll had a smart new dress, and the clockwork mouse had a splendid new hat.

"We'd better make something new for Ted!" said Jack. "We wouldn't want him to feel left out, would we!"